Simeon Bleeker's

Magical Sneakers

Written by Paul Walsh and Ronnie Nase Jr.
Illustrated by Susie Sewell

Internet addresses given in this book were accurate at the time it went to press.

Printed in the United States of America

Published in Hellertown, PA

Cover and interior design and illustrations by Susie Sewell

Control Number 2020921671

ISBN 978-1-952481-06-2

2 4 6 8 10 9 7 5 3 1 paperback

BrightCommunications.net

For all those who celebrate the differences in each other
that might not make us so different after all

This is Simeon Bleeker.

And these are his magical sneakers.

On Simeon's first day of kindergarten, he saw
many friends that he remembered from preschool.

But there was one girl who he did not remember
from preschool. She was new to Simeon's class.
Her name was Madelyn.

During reading time, Madelyn had her own
special teacher who sat right next to her.
Simeon wondered why.

During music class, Madelyn wore big headphones when no one else in the class was wearing them. Simeon wondered why.

During recess, Madelyn stood far away from the other students in Simeon's class. She held on tightly to a toy train and jumped up and down.

Simeon also liked to jump and play with toy trains.

But Madelyn just kept jumping up and down, up and down, up and down, over and over again. She never let her toy train leave her hand. Simeon wondered why.

Before the end of the school day, Simeon and his classmates lined up for the First Day of School assembly. Simeon and his friends were excited to go to the assembly, but Madelyn was not.

Madelyn stayed seated at her table next to her special teacher. She did not line up with her classmates. Instead, she cried and yelled. Simeon wondered why.

Simeon thought about Madelyn during his entire bus ride home.

Simeon thought about Madelyn on his
entire walk home from the bus stop.

When Simeon arrived home, he ran right up to his bedroom, wearing his magical sneakers.

Simeon sat at the end of his bed, gazing down at his magical sneakers. He closed his eyes and said,

"I WISH TO FEEL WHAT THEY FEEL. I WISH TO DO WHAT THEY DO. I WISH TO LEARN WHAT MAKES THEM SPECIAL JUST BY WEARING THEIR SHOES."

After speaking these words, Simeon found himself at the beginning of the school day. But this time, he experienced the day as Madelyn. Simeon's magical sneakers turned into Madelyn's shoes, and he was able to feel what Madelyn felt!

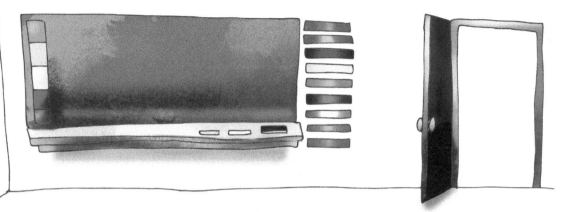

Simeon sat in reading class. Madelyn's special teacher sat right next to him. The teacher helped him follow along in the book and helped him sound out words he did not know.

"He helps Madelyn with her reading," Simeon thought. "I need help with my math sometimes. This must be why Madelyn has her special teacher who sits next to her in reading class."

Simeon was now in music class and wore Madelyn's big headphones on his ears. He took the headphones off his ears for a moment, but the music playing was far too loud. His ears were sensitive to the noise, and he could not concentrate on what the teacher was saying.

"Sometimes I need different things to help me concentrate. My glasses help me concentrate by helping me focus on the words in front of me," Simeon thought. "This must be why Madelyn needs to wear these big headphones during music class."

Simeon was now at recess. He felt overwhelmed and over excited. He held Madelyn's toy train and jumped up and down, up and down, up and down, over and over again, just like Madelyn.

"Holding this toy train makes me feel calmer, and jumping up and down helps me get my energy out. Sometimes I play with my own toy train to calm down, and I like to play soccer to help get my energy out," Simeon thought. "This must be why Madelyn holds her toy train and jumps up and down at recess."

Simeon now sat at Madelyn's table, next to her special teacher. All of the other boys and girls were lined up and ready to walk to the First Day of School assembly. Simeon felt upset. His heart raced, and he began to rock back and forth. He was not planning on going to an assembly today.

"I sometimes cry and yell when I have to do things that I did not plan on doing," Simeon thought. "Madelyn did not plan on the assembly being the next part of her day. This must be why Madelyn was so upset about going to the assembly."

Simeon opened his eyes. He learned so much about how Madelyn felt during her school day just by wearing her shoes!

The next morning, Simeon got ready for school. He got dressed, brushed his teeth, and ate his breakfast. He also grabbed his toy train before leaving his house to get on the school bus.

At recess later in the day, Simeon saw Madelyn across the schoolyard. She was holding her toy train and jumping up and down just like she did at recess yesterday.

Simeon knew this was because Madelyn was feeling just like he felt when he spent the day in her shoes.

He walked across the schoolyard
toward Madelyn, holding his toy train.

"Hello," Simeon said to Madelyn.
"Would you like to play toy trains with me?"

"Trains, trains!" Madelyn exclaimed with a smile.

Simeon began jumping right next to Madelyn. They held tightly to their toy trains. Together, they jumped up and down, up and down, up and down, over and over again until the recess bell rang.

Have you ever met someone different than you?
A person you thought about and wished that you knew?

You can get to know them if only you choose
to learn how to use your own magic shoes.

But your magic shoes are not on your feet.
They live in your heart with each little beat.

Your shoes get to work when you try to see
the world through the eyes of the people you meet.

And when all of us do this, it will be easy to see
just all we can do and all we can be.

A NOTE FROM THE AUTHORS AND ILLUSTRATOR

The three of us have been friends for quite some time. The thing that we value most about our friendship is that it is rooted in acceptance. This is why we came together to create the *Simeon Bleeker's Magical Sneakers* children's book series. We wanted to instill in children that the best relationships start with a true understanding of one another's unique perspective. We believe that tolerance and understanding are the keys to making our world a place where every person has the ability to achieve greatness.

To those of you who guide children, we hope that our books allow you to start important conversations with them about the value of seeing the world from the perspective of each person they meet, no matter their differences. In reading our books with your children, we hope you are reminded to do the same.

Always remember: Instilling the value of empathy in children begins with you. Lead by example. Show them what it means to live a life of tolerance. And as they follow your lead, our world will become just a bit brighter, lit up by the fire of kindness.

We would like to acknowledge our parents. Without your undying support of this project, Simeon Bleeker would never have had the chance to begin this magical journey.

Paul and Lori Walsh

Mark and Kathy Sewell

Ron Sr. and Fran Nase

We thank you, we admire you, and we love you.

We would also like to acknowledge our long-time friend, Don Zeman. Without your help, we would have never been able to get Soul Perspective LLC. off the ground.

Lastly, we would thank David Burns and his company, Push Play Productions LLC. Without your cinematic talent, we would have never been able to spread the message of our company and Simeon Bleeker in such a visually powerful way.

ABOUT THE AUTHORS AND ILLUSTRATOR

Paul has been a lover of words for as long he can remember. He has taught creative writing and literature for the past ten years at a high school for the arts in Bethlehem, Pennsylvania, and serves as the Artistic Director of the Literary Arts at the school. Paul holds his Master's in English Literature and is currently a doctoral student in the field of education with a focus on transformational teaching and learning. He has served as a resident poet for an online literary arts magazine and is also the author of *Lemonade*, his first novel that was published in 2019. The publication of *Simeon Bleeker's Magical Sneakers* marks Paul's authorial debut in the genre of children's books.

Ronnie graduated from Kutztown University with a B.S. in Electronic Media/Speech Communication. Ronnie's eight years of experience serving children in the mental health field truly speak to his passion for spreading empathy to those young and old. During that time, Ronnie has served his community as a Mental Health Technician, Therapeutic Staff Support, Respite Care Worker, and Special Education Instructional Assistant. He is excited to be working with his best friends on his authorial debut of *Simeon Bleeker's Magical Sneakers.*

Susie has had a passion for creativity since a very young age. She is an artist with backgrounds in multiple fields including glass blowing, painting, and illustration. She holds a Bachelor's in Fine Arts degree with a concentration in Glass and a Minor in Art History from Tyler School of Art, Temple University. She also holds an Associates in Applied Science for Communication Design from Northampton Area Community College. This is Susie's illustrative debut in the genre of children's books.